# Be a Kid Physicist

## William R. Wellnitz, Ph.D.

**TAB Books**
Division of McGraw-Hill, Inc.
Blue Ridge Summit, PA 17294-0850

FIRST EDITION
FIRST PRINTING

© 1993 by **TAB Books**.
TAB Books is a division of McGraw-Hill, Inc.

**Library of Congress Cataloging-in-Publication Data**
Wellnitz, William R., 1949-
    Be a kid physicist / by William R. Wellnitz.
       p.    cm.
    Includes index.
    Summary: Presents experiments that use materials found around the home and explore the principles of light, electricity, magnetism, motion, heat, and sound.
    ISBN 0-8306-4091-6      ISBN 0-8306-4092-4 (pbk.)
    1. Physics—Experiments—Juvenile literature.    [1. Physics-
-Experiments.    2. Experiments.]    I. Title.
QC25.W36   1993
530′.078—dc20                                        92-40506
                                                          CIP
                                                          AC

Acquisitions Editor: Kimberly Tabor
Book Editor: April Nolan
Production team:    Katherine G. Brown, Director
                    Susan E. Hansford, Typesetting
                    Lisa M. Mellott, Layout
                    Nancy Mickley, Proofreading
                    Kristine D. Lively-Helman, Indexer
                    Donna M. Gladhill, Quality Control
Design team: Jaclyn J. Boone, Designer
            Brian Allison, Associate Designer
Special thanks to Janice Lebeyka for her illustrations.                    KIDS

## Dedication

To my parents for encouraging my curiosity
and to my mother-in-law for telling me to
stop writing novels.

## Acknowledgments

Thanks to my family—my wife, Dianne, for a little of every-thing, my son Shane for the illustrations, and my daughter Cassie and my son Joshua for serving as models in the photos. Thanks also to Valerie Spratlin for the photographs and to Kim Tabor and April Nolan of Tab Books for suggestions.

# Contents

---

* Possible science fair experiments

# SOUND

# ELECTRICITY & MAGNETISM

# LIGHT

---

* Possible science fair experiments

## HEAT

# Notes to children

I wrote this book so you could have fun with science. Your kitchen or yard can become your own science laboratory. You don't need fancy equipment. Almost everything you need should be found in your home.

Physics is the branch of science that deals with light, motion, heat, sound, electricity, and magnetism. Many areas of physics overlap each other. For example, electric currents can produce magnetic fields. Motion can produce sound, heat, and sometimes light.

Look through the book and find one or two experiments you find interesting. (Each experiment tells you at the beginning what happens.) Gather all the materials you will need for the experiment, and keep the materials in one place.

Before beginning, be sure to read the section, *Symbols Used in This Book*. Become familiar with the meanings of the symbols. They provide you with all the safety precautions you should practice. Pay special attention to whether you should have an adult present when you do the experiment. Always keep safety in mind when doing any science experiment.

When you are ready to start an experiment, first read the procedure, but do not read the explanation until you have done the experiment. Then complete the experiment, following the directions exactly as they are written. Look at the pictures to be sure you have set things up correctly.

Use all of your senses as you observe what happens. If you must write something down, such as a measurement, do it as soon as you make the measurement. Your memory is often not as good as it seems.

Try to explain what happened and why. You might want to repeat the experiment one or two more times. Now look at the explanation to see if you figured it out. Try to talk about the experiment with an adult.

After you have done the experiment, try changing some of the materials and experiment on your own. Be curious! Have fun! Be safe!

If you have questions or did some new and interesting things, or would just like to comment on the book, please write to me:

Dr. Bill Wellnitz
Biology Department
Augusta College
Augusta, Georgia 30910

# Notes to adults

This book, like its predecessors, had its origin with my children. Many times when they had friends over, rather than making cookies, we would do science experiments in the kitchen. Our kitchen became a wonderful laboratory, and soon the number of children wanting to do kitchen science exceeded the space of our kitchen. The demand for science experiments and experience quickly grew into three weekend continuing-education science classes for children at Augusta College.

Physics is the branch of science that deals with light, electricity, magnetism, motion, heat, and sound. These areas are not separate entities but often overlap. For example, motion often produces sound, heat, and sometimes light.

The intent of this book is threefold:

1. To expose children to principles and procedures of physics
2. To show children that science, and especially physics, is and can be fun
3. To stimulate thinking and creativity

By showing young children that science is fun, I hope to encourage them to maintain an interest in and an appreciation for science.

Understanding scientific concepts requires active participation, but it is not necessary to use sophisticated equipment. Stimulating creative thinking often involves exposure to a discrepant, or surprising, event. Convincing children that science is fun demands that they be allowed to play and experiment on their own.

Consequently, the simple, safe experiments in this book:

- Use items that are readily available in the home
- Often appear as magic tricks
- Are open-ended

All experiments have been "kid-tested" many times, and most require less than 30 minutes to complete.

Although most experiments can be done by children alone, I encourage you to become involved—but only as a guide. Some experiments demand your assistance and should not be done by children alone. These experiments require the use of a stove, flames, or electricity; such experiments are clearly indicated by the icons at the start of each experiment.

Help the children find the materials they will need, but let them do the experiment themselves. Discuss the results with them, and encourage them to think of explanations and other uses of the process involved.

Two important aspects of science are observation and measurement. Encourage your children to use all their senses, to measure accurately, and to record their observations. For some experiments, I have provided graphs to show children how to present results.

Many of the experiments are intentionally open-ended. Children are naturally curious and will want to vary the procedure or try different materials. Don't become alarmed if they do this; just make certain they do the experiment as written on their first attempt. Many a great discovery has come from someone modifying an existing procedure.

Each of the six parts in the book begins with a brief description of the area of physics the children will explore through completing the experiments that follow. Also included in this introductory material is a list of "important words," the definitions of which can all be found in the glossary. Encourage the children to learn these words and to expand their scientific vocabulary.

The experiments in this book provide a solid background in scientific principles and methodology, and the techniques can easily be applied to other situations. Some of the experiments, with expansion and modification, could easily become science fair projects. While my intent is not to provide a listing of science fair projects, those experiments that would make good potential science fair projects are indicated by * in the table of contents. If your child does a science fair project, be sure that he or she actually does the work.

Finally, you might find you enjoy many of the experiments; and if you have a fear of science, you, too, may discover that science can be fun. I welcome your comments, both positive and negative; my address appears in *Notes to Children*.

# Symbols used in this book

adult
supervision

fire

electricity

scissors

sharp object

stove

safety
goggles

dangerous
chemical

# Part 1
# Motion

Why do objects move? Some move because something pushes or pulls them. Others move because something else that is moving collides with a nonmoving object. As an object moves, it begins to slow down because of *friction*, which is the rubbing together of two or more objects, usually resulting in the object slowing down or becoming hotter. In this section you will examine different aspects of motion.

**important words**
- ☆ friction
- ☆ gravity
- ☆ inclined plane
- ☆ inertia
- ☆ pendulum

# 1
# Colliding & moving balls

**objective** ☆   A moving ball will stop and a stopped ball will begin to move.

**materials** ☆
- ❑ 4 straws
- ❑ tape
- ❑ book
- ❑ 8 to 10 same-sized marbles

**procedure** ☆
1. Use small pieces of tape to attach two of the straws together. Be sure to put tape on only one side of the straw. Make two sets of straws.
2. Place one set of straws on the counter. Be sure the taped side is down.
3. Place the other set of straws so that one end rests on the book. The other end of the straws should just touch the straws on the table.

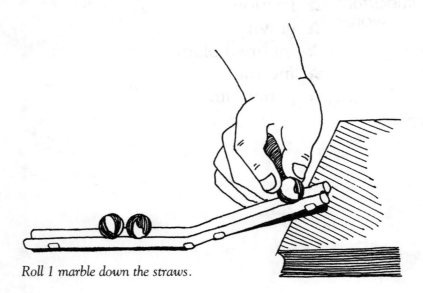

*Roll 1 marble down the straws.*

4. Place 2 marbles in the middle of the straws on the table. These marbles must be touching.
5. Hold another marble at the top of the sloped straws and release this marble. How many marbles moved?
6. Place 3 or 4 marbles on the flat straws. Be sure all marbles are touching.
7. Hold 2 marbles together on the sloped straws and release them. How many marbles moved this time?
8. Try other combinations of marbles on each set of straws.

*Roll 2 marbles down the straws.*

**explanation** ☆ Motion is a type of energy. The energy in the moving marbles is transferred to the nonmoving marble, causing it to move. This energy will move through many nonmoving marbles until it reaches the end marble. You have probably seen toys with balls hanging on strings. You can make these balls move back and forth because of this rule.

# 2
# Moving a penny from a stack

**objective** ☆ Bet a friend that you can move the bottom penny from a stack without touching the stack.

**materials** ☆ ☐ about 10 or 15 pennies, same-sized buttons, or checkers

**procedure** ☆ 1. Make a stack of 5 to 10 pennies.

*Make a stack of coins.*

2. Place another penny on the table, about 2 inches (5 cm) from the stack.
3. Use your finger to flick the penny so that it moves straight into the stack. You might have to try this step a few times.
4. What happened to the penny at the bottom of the stack?

**explanation** ☆ The law of *inertia* says that an object in motion tends to stay in motion and an object at rest tends to stay at rest. The stack of pennies was at rest. The energy of the moving penny was transferred to the bottom penny, and it moved.

For similar experiments, see experiments 1 and 3.

*Watch a single coin hit the stack of coins.*

# 3
# Making a stopped ball move

**objective** ☆ A ball sitting in a moving wagon rolls forward when the wagon stops.

**materials** ☆ ☐ wagon
☐ ball

**procedure** ☆ 1. Place the ball inside the wagon, near the rear.

*Place a ball at the back of the wagon.*

2. Pull the wagon for a few seconds.
3. Suddenly stop the wagon.
4. Notice the position of the ball when the wagon stops.

**explanation** ☆ The ball and the wagon were both moving. When the wagon stopped, the ball kept moving. This experiment is another example of *inertia*. A similar thing happens when a car suddenly

*Pull the wagon, then stop.*

stops. The passenger is usually thrown forward. A seat belt helps to keep the person from hitting his or her head on the window.

The rules of inertia were discovered over 300 years ago by Isaac Newton.

# 4
# Racing bottles & cans

**objective** ☆  You will race different-sized containers down a ramp.

**materials** ☆
- ☐ large piece of plywood or cardboard, at least 3 feet × 2 feet (1 meter × 0.67 meter)
- ☐ large plastic soft drink bottle with lid
- ☐ small soft drink bottle with lid
- ☐ empty soft drink can
- ☐ full, unopened soft drink can
- ☐ steps, or books to make a pile 8–12 inches (20–30 cm) high
- ☐ water from faucet

**procedure** ☆  1. Place one end of the plywood on the steps to make a ramp.

*Set up a ramp.*

2. Hold the empty and full soft drink cans at the top of the ramp. Be sure they are far enough apart that they will not collide as they roll down the ramp.
3. Release both cans at the same time. Which one reached the bottom first?
4. Place the empty small and large bottles at the top of the ramp. Release them at the same time. Which one reached the bottom first?

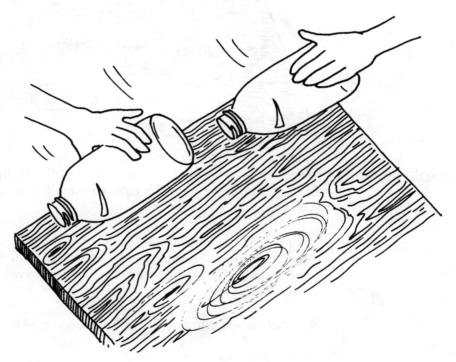

*Roll empty bottles down the ramp.*

5. Fill both bottles with water and put on the lids.
6. Place the full bottles at the top of the ramp. Which bottle do you think will reach the bottom first? Why?
7. Release both bottles. Was your idea correct? You might want to repeat this last race one or two more times.

*Roll full bottles down the ramp.*

**explanation** ☆ Objects roll down hills because *gravity* pulls on them. The large, empty bottle traveled faster than the small, empty bottle because it was heavier.

You probably thought that the large filled bottle would travel faster than the small filled one. The water in the bottle created more *friction* as it rolled, so it traveled more slowly than the small filled bottle.

For another experiment with friction, see experiment 5.

# 5
# Moving marbles

**objective** ☆  You will determine which materials will slow down a moving marble.

**materials** ☆
- ❏ 2 straws
- ❏ tape
- ❏ book
- ❏ ruler with centimeter divisions
- ❏ cookie sheet
- ❏ sandpaper, at least 6 inches (15 cm) long
- ❏ piece of cloth and piece of carpet, each about 6 inches (15 cm) long
- ❏ marble or small ball
- ❏ water from faucet
- ❏ freezer
- ❏ pencil & paper

**procedure** ☆
1. Put water in the cookie sheet and place it in the freezer until it freezes.
2. Tape 2 straws together. Put the tape only on one side.
3. Place one end of the straw on the book in order to make a ramp.
4. Place the ruler on the counter. The end of the ruler should be even with the end of the straw.
5. Hold the marble at the top of the ramp and let it roll down the ramp.
6. Measure how far the marble traveled, and record this distance.
7. Place the piece of sandpaper at the end of the ramp. Repeat steps 5 and 6.
8. Place the cloth at the end of the ramp. Repeat steps 5 and 6.
9. Place the sheet of ice in the cookie sheet at the end of the ramp. Repeat steps 5 and 6.
10. Put your results on a graph like the one shown here.

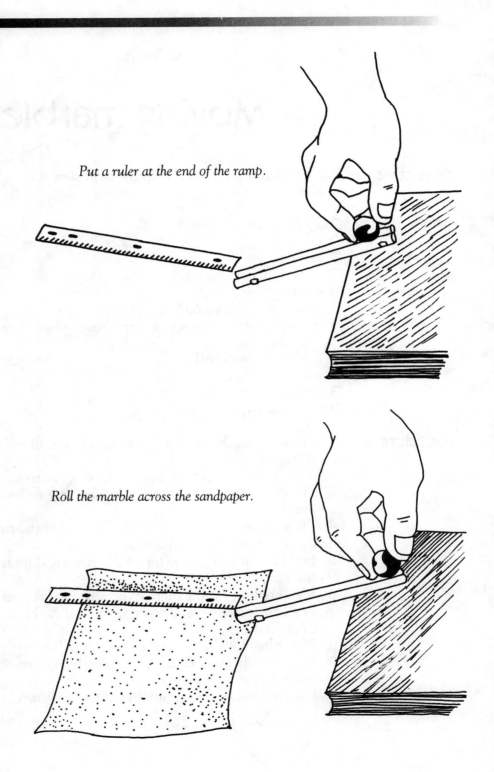

Put a ruler at the end of the ramp.

Roll the marble across the sandpaper.

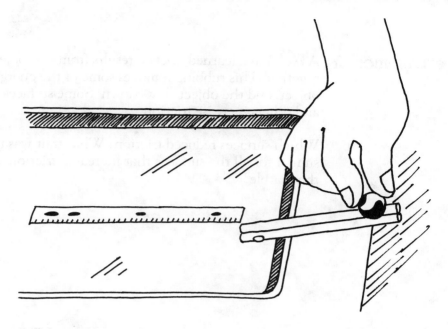

*Roll the marble across the ice.*

DISTANCE (CM)

*A graph for distance traveled.*

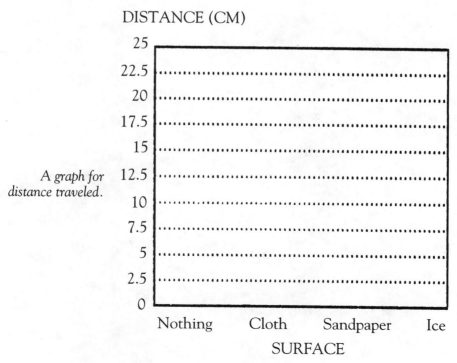

**explanation** ☆ As you have learned, *friction* results from two objects rubbing together. This rubbing removes some of the energy of a moving object, and the object slows down. Some surfaces reduce friction and others increase friction.

Which surfaces reduced friction? What trait was the same or similar for all the surfaces that increased friction and slowed down the marble?

# 6
# Moving an object up a hill

**objective** ☆ You will pull an object up different slopes.

**materials** ☆
- [ ] books or pieces of wood, enough to make a pile 6 to 8 inches (15 to 20 cm) high
- [ ] strip of wood 12 inches (30 cm) long (strips of cardboard also work)
- [ ] strip of wood 3 feet (1 meter) long
- [ ] rubber band
- [ ] block of wood or other object about 2 inches (5 cm) on each side

**procedure** ☆
1. Stack the books or wood to make a stack 6 to 8 inches (15 to 20 cm) high.
2. Make 2 ramps with the 2 strips of wood, from the stack of books to the tabletop.
3. Place the rubber band around the block, and place the block at the bottom of one ramp.

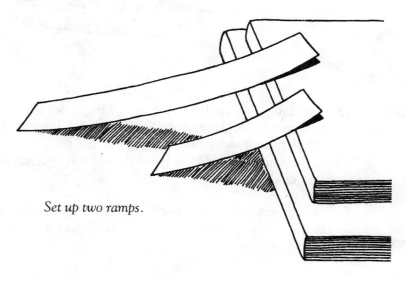

*Set up two ramps.*

4. Slowly pull the rubber band until the block begins to move. You must pull in the same direction as the ramp.
5. Now place the block at the end of the second ramp.
6. Pull the rubber band until the block begins to move.
7. Did the rubber band stretch the same amount on each ramp? On which ramp did the rubber band stretch more?

*Pull the block with a rubber band.*

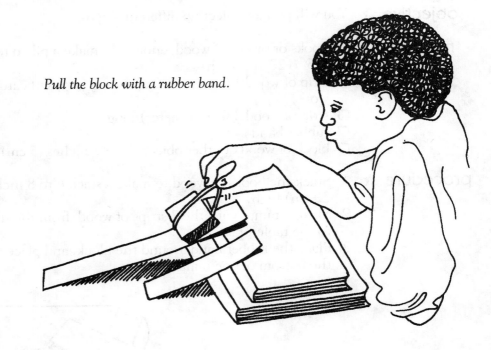

**explanation** ☆ The ramp is actually an *inclined plane*, a device that makes it easier to move an object to a certain height. A long slope requires less effort than a short, steep slope, but the total amount of work done is the same. The rubber band should have stretched less on the longer slope.

Based on what you learned from this experiment, why do you think roads up mountains curve back and forth so many times?

# 7
# Making parachutes

**objective** ☆   You will try to make the best parachute. This experiment is best done with two or more people.

**materials** ☆  
- ❏ many paper napkins
- ❏ many pieces of string, each about 15 inches (38 cm) long
- ❏ metal washer
- ❏ watch with second hand
- ❏ pencil & paper

**procedure** ☆  
1. Open a napkin and carefully tie one piece of string to each of the corners. Be careful not to rip the napkin.

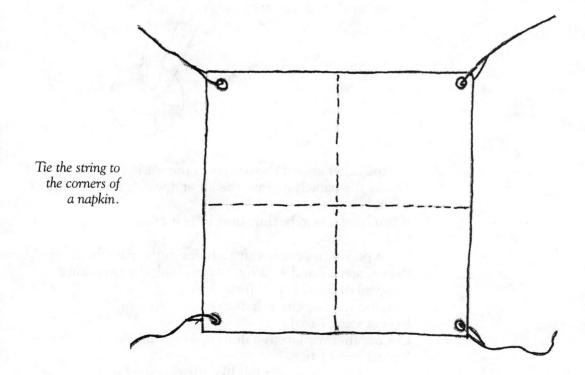

*Tie the string to the corners of a napkin.*

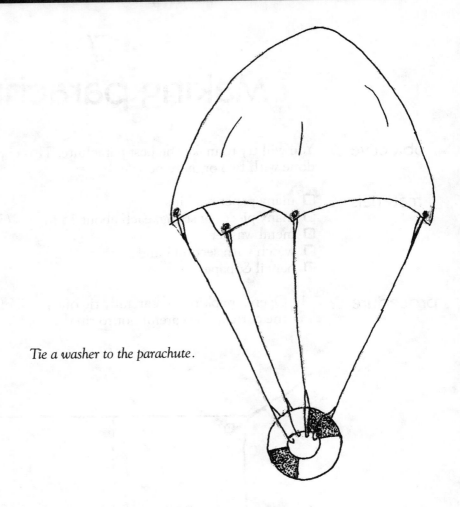

*Tie a washer to the parachute.*

2. Tie the other end of the strings to the washer.
3. Throw the parachute into the air and watch it fall to the ground.
4. If you have a watch, time how long it takes the parachute to fall.
5. Use a pencil to punch 4 small holes in the parachute.
6. Repeat steps 3 and 4. Why do you think the parachute behaved differently this time?
7. Cut another napkin in half to make a rectangle.
8. Repeat steps 1 to 4.
9. Cut another napkin in half to make a triangle.
10. Repeat steps 1 to 4.
11. Put your results on a graph like the one shown here.

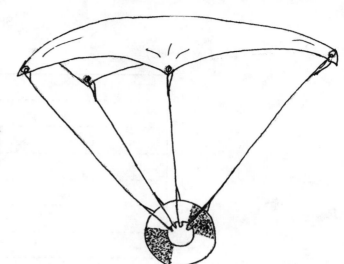

*A rectangular parachute.*

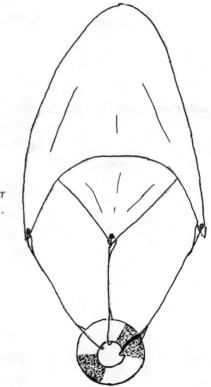

*A triangular parachute.*

SHAPES OF
PARACHUTES

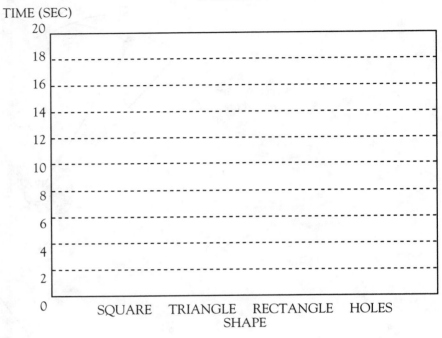

TIME (SEC)

| | SQUARE | TRIANGLE | RECTANGLE | HOLES |

SHAPE

**explanation** ☆ A parachute works by using *drag* or *friction* to slow down a falling object. Which shape worked best in slowing the fall? Try many other different shapes—such as a circle, star, etc.—to see how they behave.

# 8
# Dropping balls

**objective** ☆    You will drop different-sized balls to see which one hits the ground first. This experiment requires two or more people.

**materials** ☆    ❑ 2 balls of different size (for example: a basketball and a tennis ball) OR use 2 different-sized stones
      ❑ high place, such as a second-story window

**procedure** ☆    1. One person should stay on the ground and the other should climb to the second-story window, taking both balls with him or her.
      2. Hold both balls at the same height and drop them at the same time.

*Hold two different balls at the same height.*

*Release the balls at
the same time.*

3. The person on the ground should determine which ball—if either—hits the ground first.

**explanation** ☆ You were probably surprised that both balls hit at the same time. You probably thought the heavier ball would hit first. *Gravity* causes the balls to fall, and gravity exerts the same force on all objects. The heavier ball hits the ground harder, but it falls at the same rate as the lighter ball.

This is the experiment the famous scientist Galileo did over 300 years ago. For another experiment on falling objects, see experiment 7.

# 9
# The swinging tennis ball

**objective** ☆  You can hold a ball on a string near your nose but not get hit with the swinging ball.

**materials** ☆  ❑ tape
❑ tennis ball, orange, or lemon
❑ string, at least 6 feet (2 meters) long

**procedure** ☆  1. Tape one end of the string to the tennis ball. Be sure that the string is firmly attached to the ball.
2. Tie the other end of the string to a branch, or have an adult tape it to the ceiling.
3. Adjust the string so that it hangs to the height of your nose.
4. Take 1 or 2 steps backward so the ball is no longer hanging straight up and down.
5. Hold the ball next to your nose and let it go. *Note: Do not push the ball.*
6. Stand still as the ball swings. (Don't worry; it will not hit you.)

**explanation** ☆  An object on a string that swings back and forth is called a *pendulum.* As a pendulum swings, it never returns to its starting point unless it is pulled or pushed by some force. The air around the pendulum pushes on it and slows it down.

When you are on a swing on a playground, you are using a pendulum. Unless you move your body, you will never go as high as your first swing. Can you think of other examples of pendulums?

*Hold the ball to your nose.*

*Release the ball.*

# 10
# A dancing balloon

**objective** ☆ A coin inside a balloon makes the balloon dance in unusual ways.

**materials** ☆ ☐ large balloon
☐ coin

**procedure** ☆ 1. Place the coin inside the balloon.

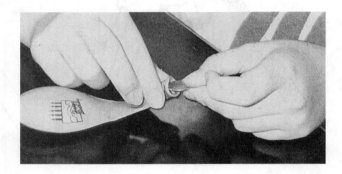

2. Blow up the balloon and tie it closed.
3. Drop the balloon. What happens?
4. Hold the balloon between your hands and start moving the balloon in a circle. The coin should start rolling around the balloon on its edge. It will take a few tries to get the proper motion of the balloon.
5. Drop the balloon. What happens?
6. Repeat step 4, and carefully place the balloon on a table. What happens?

**explanation** ☆ As the coin moves around the balloon, it creates a force on the side of the balloon. Because the coin is never in one place, it pushes on the balloon in different directions, making it hop around when dropped.

For another experiment with coins in a balloon, see experiment 26.

*Swirl the balloon quickly.*

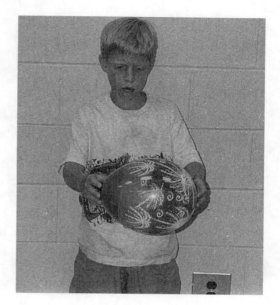

*Release the balloon.*

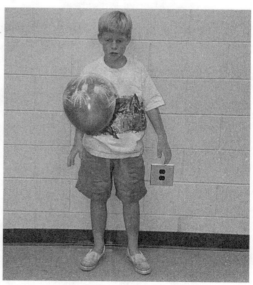

# Part 2
# Air & water

Air is all around us. It takes up space and has weight. It expands when heated and contracts when cooled. It pushes on things and can make them move.

Water is a clear, colorless, tasteless liquid. Water can be made to move by air pushing on it.

**important words**

☆ contract
☆ expand
☆ molecule
☆ siphon

# 11
# A shrinking balloon

**objective** ☆  An inflated balloon will shrink. This experiment will take about 30 minutes.

**materials** ☆
- ❒ balloon
- ❒ Styrofoam cup
- ❒ refrigerator

**procedure** ☆
1. Place the balloon inside the cup.
2. Holding the cup with one hand, blow up the balloon until the balloon pushes on the walls of the cup. The balloon should be blown up enough to allow you to pick up the cup by lifting the balloon.
3. Tie the end of the balloon in a knot. You should still be able to pick up the cup.
4. Place the balloon-cup in the refrigerator for about 30 minutes.
5. After 30 minutes, examine the balloon. Can you still pick up the cup with it?

**explanation** ☆  Warm air *expands*, or takes up more space. Cold air *contracts*, or shrinks. When you placed the balloon in the refrigerator, the air inside the balloon contracted, and the balloon no longer pushed against the sides of the cup.

What do you think will happen if you leave the cold balloon in the cup at room temperature for a while? Try it to see if you are right.

*Place the inflated balloon-cup in the refrigerator.*

*Take the balloon out of the refrigerator after 30 minutes.*

Be a Kid Physicist

# 12
# Air has weight

**objective** ☆  You will show that air has weight.

**materials** ☆
- ❏ 3 straws
- ❏ pin or paper clip
- ❏ 2 balloons the same size
- ❏ 2 pieces of string, about 6 inches (15 cm) long
- ❏ 1 piece of string, about 12 inches (30 cm) long

**procedure** ☆

1. Make a **T** with the two straws. Hold them together with a pin. (Be careful not to stick yourself!)
2. Loosely tie the short strings to the balloons.
3. Tie the balloons to the stick about 1 inch (2.5 cm) from each end.
4. Grasp the vertical straw so the straw with the balloons hangs freely. The straw should be balanced. If it is not, move one of the balloons until the straw is balanced and horizontal.

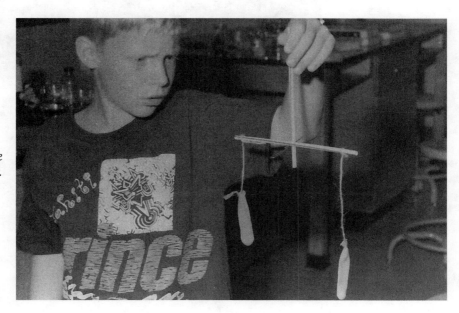

*Making a simple scale or balance.*

5. Remove one balloon and blow it up. Tie the balloon closed.
6. Retie the string to the balloon and attach the inflated balloon to the simple balance.
7. Repeat step 4. Is one side now heavier?

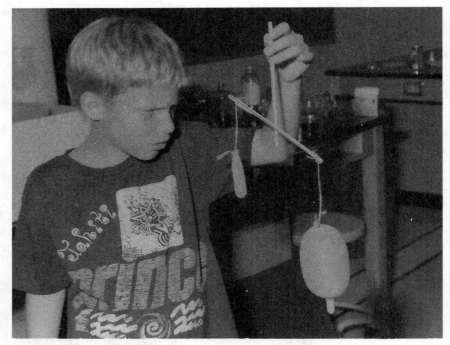

*Place an inflated balloon on one end.*

**explanation** ☆ Air has weight. When you blew up the balloon, you put more air into the balloon, so it became heavier and tilted the straw.

# 13
# Emptying a bottle

**objective** ☆  When you punch a hole in a plastic bottle, water may come out at different speeds. *Note:* This experiment must be done over the sink.

**materials** ☆  ❏ 2 plastic soft-drink or milk bottles with lids
❏ scissors or knife (for the adult to use)
❏ water from faucet
❏ watch with a second hand (optional)

**procedure** ☆  1. Fill both bottles with water.
2. Put the lid on one bottle and hold the bottle over the sink.

3. With the scissors, punch a hole in the bottle near the bottom. If you are using a knife, have the adult do this for you.

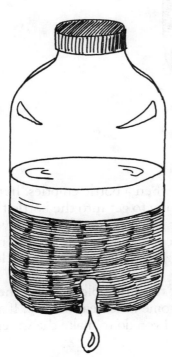

*Water leaving a closed container.*

4. Observe how fast the water leaves the bottle. Does the bottle empty completely?
5. Repeat steps 3 and 4, but use a bottle without a lid. Did this bottle empty completely?

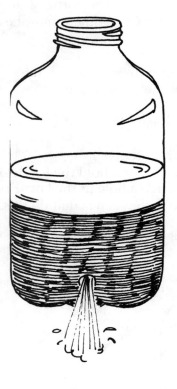

*Water leaving an open container.*

**explanation** ☆ Air replaces the water when a bottle empties. In the first experiment, air was trying to get into the bottle through the same opening that the water was leaving. This air prevented the water from leaving. In the second experiment, air entered from the top and pushed onto the top of the water, making it leave faster.

Water jugs make use of this principle. Most of them have a spout for the water and also some hole near the top. If a jug does not have a hole, what could you do to make the water come out easier?

# 14
# Removing water without pouring

**objective** ☆    You will move water from one jar to another without pouring the water. *Note:* This experiment must be done over the sink.

**materials** ☆   
- ❏ 2 jars the same size
- ❏ plastic or rubber tubing, about 15 inches (38 cm) long (available in pet stores)
- ❏ water from faucet
- ❏ pan

**procedure** ☆   
1. Fill one jar ¾ full with water.
2. Turn a pan upside down and place it on the counter near the sink.
3. Place the jar of water on top of the pan. Place the empty jar in the sink.
4. Fill the tube completely with water from the faucet. Pinch both ends of the tube to keep water from coming out.
5. Place one end of the tube in the jar with water and place the other end in the empty jar.
6. Unpinch the ends of the tubing and watch what happens to the water. If the water does not move from one jar to the other, try this:

   - Remove the tube and empty any water into the sink.
   - Place one end of the tube in the jar with water.
   - Suck water into the tube.
   - Quickly put the other end of the tube into the empty jar.

**explanation** ☆    The device you have made is called a *siphon*. Gravity causes water to move from a higher place to a lower place. As the water leaves the tube, air pushes on the water in the jar and forces more water into the tube, thus emptying the jar. Can you think of any uses of siphons?

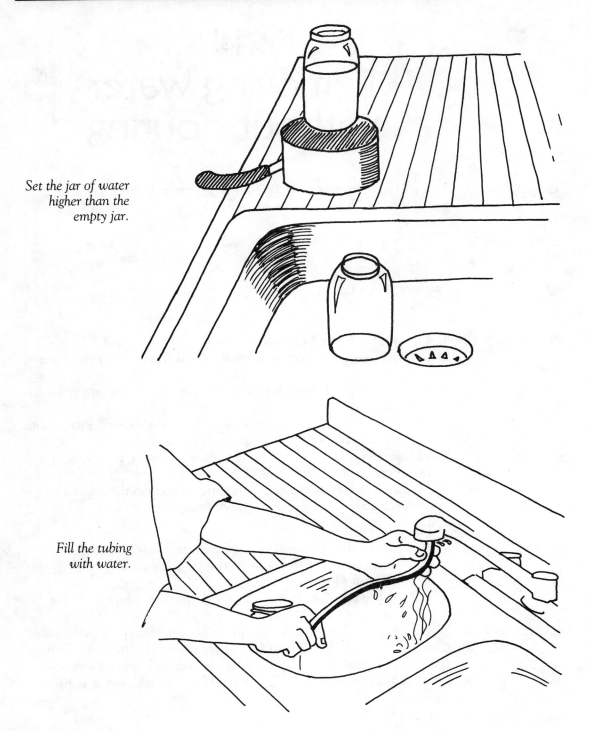

Set the jar of water higher than the empty jar.

Fill the tubing with water.

Place the tubing in both jars.

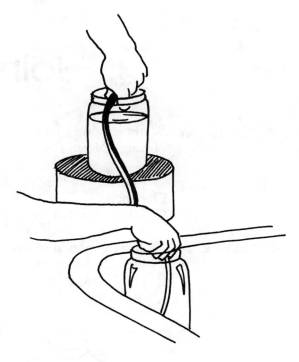

# 15
# Joining water

**objective** ☆ Water leaving a jar by many holes can be made to form one stream of water. *Note:* This experiment must be done over the sink.

**materials** ☆
- ☐ plastic milk jug or soft-drink bottle
- ☐ pencil
- ☐ water from faucet

**procedure** ☆
1. Use the pencil to punch 3 or 4 holes near the bottom of the jug. The holes should be about ¼ inch (6 mm) apart.
2. Fill the jug half-full with water. Water should form a stream from each hole.

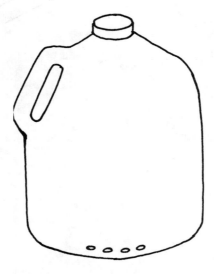

*Punch holes in a jug.*

*Water coming through the holes.*

3. With your thumb and first finger, slowly pinch the streams of water until your fingers meet.
4. Remove your finger. You should see just one stream.

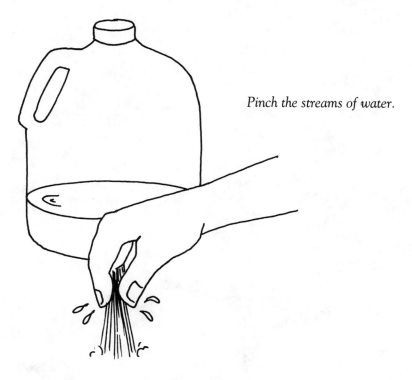

*Pinch the streams of water.*

**explanation** ☆    Water *molecules* (the smallest part of the water compound, $H_2O$, that can exist freely but still maintain all the properties of water) are held together and attracted to other water molecules. When you pinched the streams of water, the molecules in one stream were attracted to those in another stream.

# Part 3
# Sound

Sound is produced when matter moves back and forth or vibrates in the air. The vibrations cause the air to vibrate at a certain rate or *frequency*. High-frequency vibrations produce sounds that have a high *pitch* or tone. Sounds with slow vibrations are low-pitched.

For you to be able to hear a sound, the vibrating air must travel to your eardrum and cause it to vibrate. Materials that prevent sound from traveling are called *insulators*.

In this section you will look at many different properties of sounds.

**important words**

☆ amplify
☆ bass
☆ frequency
☆ insulator
☆ pitch
☆ reflect
☆ treble
☆ vibrate

# 16
# Using sound to move paper

**objective** ☆   You will show that sound is moving air by using sound from a radio speaker to make paper move.

**materials** ☆   ❏ radio with at least one speaker
          ❏ small sheet of paper, large enough to cover the speaker
          ❏ tape

**procedure** ☆   1. Tape the sheet of paper over the speaker.
          2. Turn on the radio, but keep the volume low.
          3. Slowly increase the volume. Observe what happens to the paper.

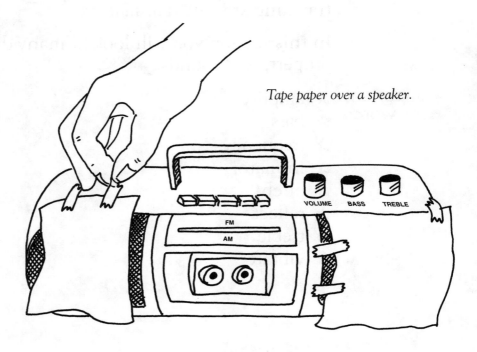

*Tape paper over a speaker.*

*Increase the volume.*

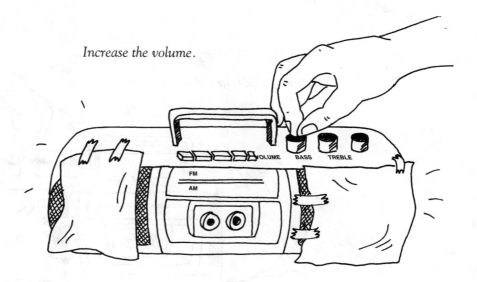

If you have controls for bass and treble, try this experiment:
1. Set the bass and treble controls in the middle.
2. Turn up the volume so you can see the paper vibrate.
3. Turn the knob to full bass, then turn the knob to full treble.

*Adjust the bass.*

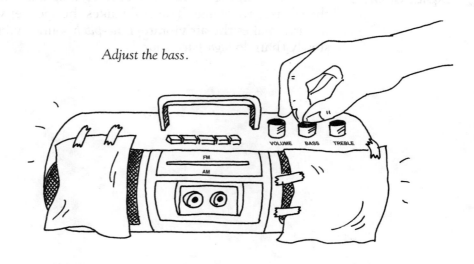

*Adjust the treble.*

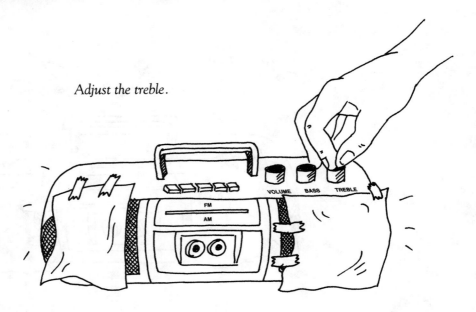

4. Does the paper vibrate at different speeds depending upon whether you are hearing bass or treble sounds?

**explanation** ☆ The wires coming to the speaker release signals that cause a coil in the speaker to *vibrate*. The coil makes the speaker vibrate, which, in turn, makes the air vibrate. *Low-pitch* sounds vibrate more slowly than do *high-pitch* sounds.

# 17
# Making a kazoo

**objective** ☆ You will make a *kazoo*, a simple musical instrument that makes an unusual sound.

**materials** ☆ ❑ comb
❑ wax paper, about 3 inches (7.5 cm) square

**procedure** ☆ 1. Hold the comb to your lips and hum. Do you hear a sound?
2. Fold the wax paper in half, hold it to your lips and hum. Do you hear a sound?

*Hold the comb to your lip.*

*Hold the wax paper to your lips.*

3. Place the comb in the folded wax paper. Place the wax paper/comb to your lips and hum. Do you hear an unusual sound? You might have to move the comb slightly until you get the sound.
4. Slide the comb back and forth as you hum, or try humming a tune. Can you make sounds with different pitches?

*Hold the kazoo to your lips.*

**explanation** ☆ Humming makes the wax paper vibrate. You might have heard some sound with just the wax paper. When the paper vibrates, it causes the teeth of the comb to vibrate, making a funny, buzzing noise. By trying each object alone, you showed that you need both objects to make the unusual sound.

# 18
# How far away is the lightning?

**objective** ☆ When you see lightning during a thunderstorm, you can estimate how far away it is.

**materials** ☆ ❏ thunderstorm
❏ watch with second hand (optional)

**procedure** ☆ 1. When you see a flash of lightning, immediately start timing or counting, "One-thousand-one, one-thousand-two," etc.
2. Keep counting until you hear the thunder.
3. Divide by 5 the number of seconds between the time you saw the lightning and the time you heard the thunder. This answer will give an estimate in miles of how far away the lightning was. If you divide the seconds by 3, you will estimate the distance in kilometers.

*Look at the lightning.*

**explanation** ☆ When lightning occurs, the bolt suddenly removes all the air around the bolt, or creates a *vacuum*. Thunder is the sound caused by the air rushing into this vacuum.

*Count until you hear thunder.*

Sound travels through air at 1,100 feet per second (about 330 meters per second). There are 5,280 feet in a mile, so in 5 seconds, sound travels just a little more than 1 mile.

# 19
# What sounds are easier to hear?

**objective** ☆ You will determine whether a high- or low-pitched sound is easier to hear. *NOTE:* This experiment works best with 2 people.

**materials** ☆ ❑ radio with bass and treble controls *OR* make high- and low-pitched sounds as in experiment 22.

**procedure** ☆ 1. Turn on the radio and stand about 3 feet (1 meter) away.
2. Adjust the volume so you can just barely hear the sound.
3. Stand sideways so one ear is toward the speaker.

*Listen to the sound.*

4. Use your finger to plug the ear that is toward the speaker. Can you still hear the sound?

5. With your finger still in your ear, have your friend turn the knob so only bass sounds come out. Can you still hear the sound? Is it softer than before?
6. Now have your friend turn the knob so only treble sounds come out. Can you hear the sound?

*If you are using glasses (as in experiment 22), do the following:*

1. Stand sideways to the glasses and stand about 3 feet (1 meter) away.
2. Plug the ear that is closer to the glasses.
3. Have a friend hit the glass that makes a low-pitched sound. Can you hear the sound?
4. Now have a friend hit the glass that makes a high-pitched sound. Can you hear the sound?

**explanation** ☆   High-pitched sounds have short waves, and low-pitched sounds have long waves. Long wavelengths can bend more easily. When you turned sideways and plugged your ear, your head and hand caused a block in the path of the sound waves. The high-pitched sounds could not bend around this block, so you probably were unable to hear the high sounds.

When you are at a parade, which sounds—those from the drum or those from the flute—do you hear first? Can you explain why?

# 20
# Bouncing sounds off objects

**objective** ☆  You will determine which objects make sounds louder or softer.

**materials** ☆
- ❏ 2 empty toilet-paper rolls
- ❏ watch
- ❏ 1 piece of wood, at least 4 inches (10 cm) square
- ❏ newspaper
- ❏ towel or other piece of cloth
- ❏ aluminum foil
- ❏ Styrofoam insulation, or many pieces of Styrofoam packing "peanuts"
- ❏ glue
- ❏ tape
- ❏ paper & pencil

**procedure** ☆
1. On a piece of paper, trace the lines shown.
2. Place the empty toilet paper rolls on the two lines. The ends of the rolls should almost touch.
3. Place the piece of wood at the ends of the rolls.
4. Place the watch at the end of one tube. Stand the watch on end.
5. Place your ear at the end of the other tube. Do you hear the watch ticking?

*Lines on which to lay the tubes.*

6. Cover the wood with aluminum foil, newspaper, or cloth.
7. Listen again for the sound of the watch. Do you hear the sound? If so, is it louder or softer than before?
8. Place a piece of Styrofoam insulation in front of the board, or glue many pieces of Styrofoam packing material on the board.
9. Listen for the watch. Do you hear it tick?
10. Try other materials to determine if they allow you to hear the sound.

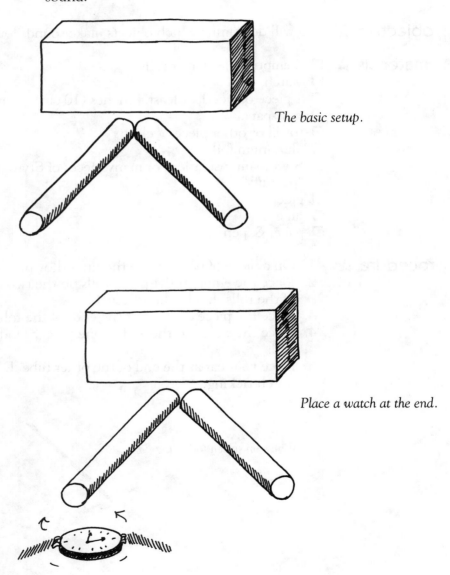

*The basic setup.*

*Place a watch at the end.*

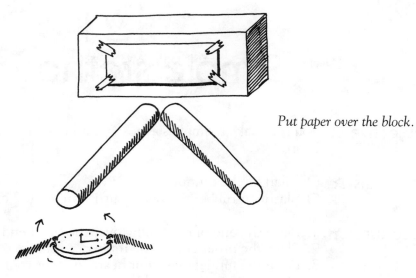

*Put paper over the block.*

**explanation** ☆ Sound from the watch traveled down the tube, bounced off the wood, and traveled down the second tube to your ear. The tube *amplified* the sound (made the sound louder) because it kept the sound in one place.

Sound bounces or is *reflected* off some materials. Other materials absorb sound and prevent it from being reflected. The latter materials make good *insulators* for sound.

Make a list of all materials that you tested that are good sound insulators. Try to determine what these materials all have in common.

# 21
# Simple stethoscope

**objective** ☆ You can make a simple stethoscope and use it to listen to your heart.

**materials** ☆ ❒ small kitchen funnel
❒ plastic or rubber tubing, about 18 inches (42 cm) long

**procedure** ☆ 1. Place the end of the tubing over the small end of the funnel.
2. Place the other end of the tubing in your ear.
3. Place the funnel over your heart (or over your partner's heart). Can you hear the sound of your heart beating?

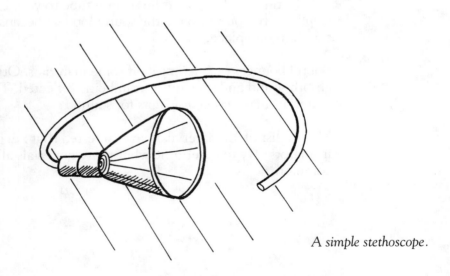

*A simple stethoscope.*

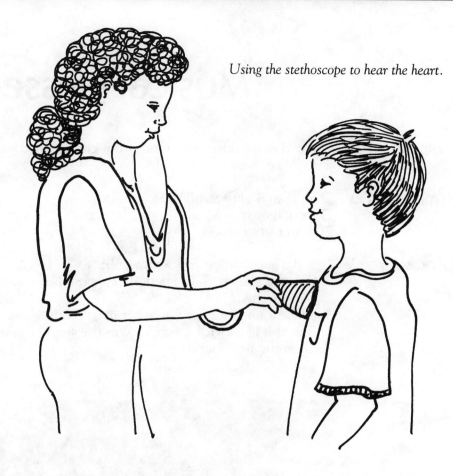

*Using the stethoscope to hear the heart.*

**explanation** ☆  The funnel served to trap the sound produced by your beating heart. This sound then traveled up the tube to your ear.

# 22
# Musical glasses

**objective** ☆ You can make different sounds from glasses filled with different amounts of water.

**materials** ☆ ☐ at least 4 glasses, all the same size
☐ pencil or spoon
☐ water from faucet

**procedure** ☆ 1. Fill a glass almost full with water.
2. Tap the glass with the pencil or spoon. Is the sound high- or low-pitched?
3. Place a small amount of water in a second glass.
4. Tap this glass with a pencil. Was the sound higher or lower than the first sound?

*Tap a full glass of water.*

*Tap an almost empty glass of water.*

5. Put different amounts of water in the other glasses. When you hit each glass, you should get a different sound.
6. Try tapping the different glasses in different orders to make a tune.

**explanation** ☆ Tapping the glass with a pencil makes the glass vibrate. The water in the glass slows down the vibrations. The air then vibrates more slowly, and air that moves slowly has a lower pitch than air that vibrates faster. What kind of glass should have the highest pitch?

For a similar experiment, see experiment 23.

# 23
# Sounds from bottles

**objective** ☆ When you blow across the top of a bottle, a sound is made. Bottles with different amounts of water will make different sounds. *NOTE:* You should do experiment 22 before doing this experiment.

**materials** ☆
- ❏ 4 or more bottles, all the same size (soft-drink bottles work well)
- ❏ water from faucet

**procedure** ☆
1. Put a small amount of water in a bottle.
2. Hold the bottle just below your bottom lip. Blow across the opening of the bottle. You might have to move the bottle slightly to get the sound. Did the sound have a high or low pitch?
3. Repeat steps 1 and 2, but with bottles that have different amounts of water in them. Which bottle produces the highest tone? The lowest tone?

*Blow across a nearly empty bottle.*

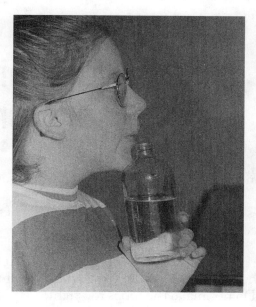

*Blow across a nearly full bottle.*

**explanation** ☆   When you blew across the bottle, some air traveled into the bottle. This air hit the water and was reflected up and back out of the bottle. When this air left the bottle, it caused more air to move into the bottle. The bottle then had air moving up and down. The air was vibrating and made a sound.

When you used the bottle with only a small amount of water, the air had to travel a long way before hitting the water. It took a long time to make the air vibrate, and a low sound was produced. Can you explain why this result is the opposite of what was obtained when you struck the bottles in experiment 22?

Air that travels a long way usually makes a low sound, and air that travels only a short distance makes a high sound. Think about a flute and a bassoon, two instruments that make sound by having air blown into them. Which ones makes a higher-pitched sound?

# 24
# The musical coat hanger

**objective** ☆ A coat hanger on a string produces an unusual sound.

**materials** ☆ ☐ 2 pieces of thread, each about 12 inches (30 cm) long
☐ metal coat hanger

**procedure** ☆ 1. Tie the pieces of string to the ends of the coat hanger.
2. Loop the other ends of the string around your fingers 2 or 3 times. Do not make the loops too tight.
3. Making sure the string loops stay on your fingers, place your fingers in your ears.
4. Bend over and gently hit the hanger on the edge of the table. Can you describe the sound?

*Wrap the string around your finger.*

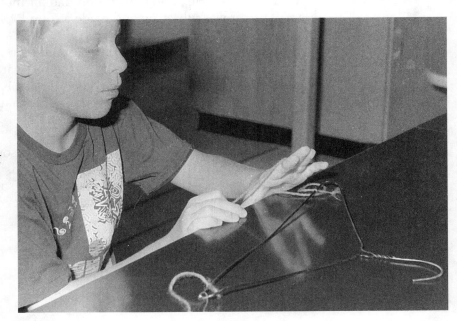

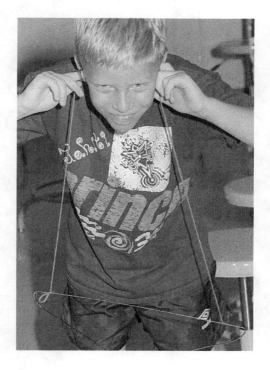

*Place your fingers in your ears.*

5. Try bending the coat hanger into a square.
6. Hit the hanger on the table again. Do you hear the same sound or a different sound?
7. Now try steps 1 to 4 with a spoon. Does it produce the same sound as the coat hanger did?

**explanation** ☆ When you hit the hanger, it starts to vibrate. The vibrations travel up the string to your ear. The sound you heard probably sounded like your head was inside a bell.

# 25
# Using sound to blow out a candle

**objective** ☆ When you thump the end of a cylindrical box, you will blow out a candle.

**materials** ☆
- ☐ empty salt box
- ☐ candle (a short, stubby one works best)
- ☐ matches

**procedure** ☆
1. Remove the metal spout from the salt container.
2. Have an adult light a candle and place the candle on the table.
3. Hold the box 2 to 3 feet (.5 to 1 meter) away from the flame.

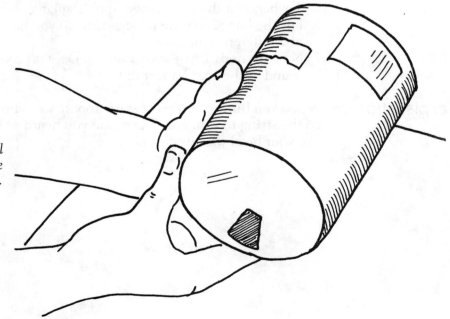

*Remove the metal spout from the salt box.*

4. Point the opening in the salt box toward the flame.
5. With your finger, thump the end of the box. You might have to try this a few times, or adjust the position of the hole. If the candle went out, move back about 1 foot (30 cm) and thump again.
6. Keep moving back until you can no longer make the flame go out.

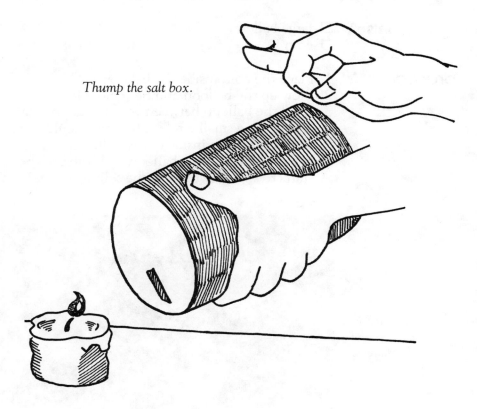

*Thump the salt box.*

**explanation** ☆ The thump created a sound, but you might not have heard it. The sound, of course, caused the air to move, and this moving air blew out the candle. How far away could you hold the box and still blow out the candle?

# 26
# Singing balloon

**objective** ☆   A coin spinning in a balloon makes different sounds.

**materials** ☆   ❑ large balloon
          ❑ coin

**procedure** ☆   1. Place the coin inside the balloon.
          2. Blow up the balloon and tie it closed.
          3. Hold the balloon between your hands and start moving the balloon in a small circle. The coin should start rolling on its edge around the inside of the balloon.
          4. Place your ear to the balloon and listen to the sound as the coin starts to slow down. Does the sound change?

*Place a coin in the balloon and inflate it.*

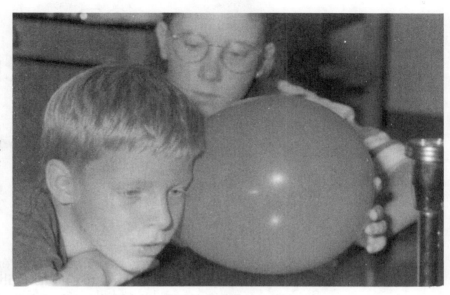

*Listen to the sound coming from inside the balloon.*

**explanation** ☆ When the coin moved fast, it caused the balloon to vibrate quickly. Objects that vibrate quickly produce a high pitch, and things that move slowly produce a low pitch.

# 27
# A dancing paper clip

**objective** ☆   You will move a paper clip on top of one glass by tapping a glass beside it.

**materials** ☆
- ❏ 2 same-sized glasses
- ❏ Water from faucet
- ❏ spoon
- ❏ paper clip

**procedure** ☆
1. Fill each glass with exactly the same amount of water. Each glass should be about one-third to one-half full.
2. Straighten the paper clip and place it on top of one of the glasses.
3. Set the other glass about 3 or 4 inches (7 to 10 cm) away from the first glass.
4. Tap the wall of the second glass with a spoon and carefully watch the paper clip. It will move a little bit.

*Fill the glasses with water.*

*Place a paper clip on one glass.*

*Hit the other glass with a spoon.*

**explanation** ☆ The glasses had the same amount of liquid in them, so the air in them vibrated at the same speed. The vibration of the first glass caused the second glass to vibrate, and this vibration made the paper clip move.

# 28
# Listening to your voice on a tape recorder

**objective** ☆ When you hear your voice on a tape recorder, it will sound different from what it sounds like to you when you talk.

**materials** ☆ ❑ tape recorder

**procedure** ☆ 1. Say a few words. How does your voice sound?
2. Now say a few words into the tape recorder and play back the tape. Does your voice sound the same as when you were speaking?

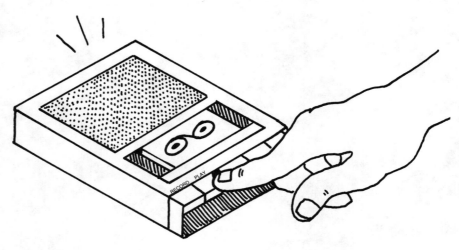

*Play back your voice.*

**explanation** ☆   When you hear someone else speak, the sound from their voice travels down your ear canal and makes your eardrum vibrate. When you speak, most of the sound that you hear comes from vibrations on the roof of your mouth. This vibration causes other vibrations in your ear. The frequency of vibration is different in air and through your mouth. The way your voice sounds on the tape recorder is how your voice sounds to other people.

# Part 4
# Electricity & magnetism

Electricity results from the movement of charges in a complete path or *circuit*. Some materials allow the charged particles to move and are called *conductors*. Other materials do not allow the charges to move and are called *insulators*. Electricity can produce magnetism and magnetism can produce electricity. Magnets will be attracted to objects that contain iron. The opposite ends or poles of magnets are attracted to each other, and like ends are repelled.

**important words**

☆ circuit
☆ conductor
☆ insulator
☆ magnetic field

# 29
# Lighting a light bulb

**objective** ☆ You will use a wire to light a flashlight bulb and test other materials to see which ones will keep the light on.

**materials** ☆
- ❏ flashlight battery
- ❏ flashlight bulb
- ❏ thin copper wire, about 12 inches (30 cm) long
- ❏ pencil
- ❏ paper clip
- ❏ thumbtack
- ❏ paper
- ❏ small piece of aluminum foil
- ❏ small strip of cloth
- ❏ small piece of plastic wrap

**procedure** ☆
1. Touch the flashlight bulb to the top of the battery. Does it light?
2. Wrap one end of the wire around the metal part of the bulb. Twist the wire tightly so the bulb won't fall out.
3. Place the other end of the wire underneath the battery.
4. Touch the bulb to the top of the battery. Why do you think the bulb lit this time but it didn't when there was no wire?
5. Hold the paper clip on top of the battery and touch the bulb to the paper clip. Does the bulb light?

*Touch the bulb to the battery.*

*Touch the bulb and wire to the battery.*

6. Remove the paper clip and touch the lead from a pencil to the top of the battery.
7. Place the bulb on top of the pencil lead. Did the bulb light? Was it as bright as when you used the paper clip?
8. Remove the pencil and place a small piece of aluminum foil on top of the battery.
9. Repeat step 7.
10. Try placing the paper or cloth between the bulb and the battery to see if the bulb will light.
11. Make a list of materials that allowed the bulb to light and a list of those materials that did not allow the bulb to light.

*Hold a paper clip between the bulb and the battery.*

**explanation** ☆   In order for electricity to move or flow, there must be a complete, closed path. In the first part of this experiment, the wire on the bottom of the battery formed a closed path or *circuit*. Electricity moved from the bottom of the battery, along the wire, to the light, and back to the battery.

Materials that allow electricity to move are called *conductors*. Some materials are weak conductors, as you saw when the bulb did not burn as brightly. Other materials that do not allow electricity to flow at all are called *insulators*. Insulators prevent the formation of a complete circuit, and the bulb does not light. What materials make good insulators? Why do you think we need insulators?

# 30
# Testing for iron

**objective** ☆ You will test different objects to see if they contain iron. Items that do contain iron will stick to a magnet.

**materials** ☆
- ❑ magnet
- ❑ stove
- ❑ pencil
- ❑ paper clip
- ❑ spoon
- ❑ aluminum foil
- ❑ pan
- ❑ paper & pencil
- ❑ tack

**Caution!** Never put a magnet near a computer, computer disk, VCR, or a television. A magnet will damage these items.

**procedure** ☆
1. Touch the magnet to the stove. Does it stick to the stove?
2. Now test a spoon to see if it will stick to a magnet.
3. Touch the magnet to the other different objects.
4. Make a list of those objects that contain iron and those that do not.

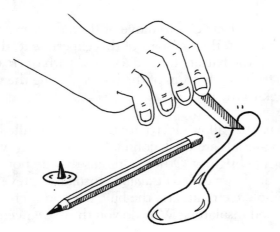

*Touch the magnet to a metal object.*

**explanation** ☆   A magnet will stick to things that contain iron. Some metals, such as steel, contain iron, but other metals, such as aluminum foil, do not.

# 31
# Observing a magnetic field

**objective** ☆ You will be able to see how the force lines of a magnet are arranged.

**materials** ☆
- ❑ nail
- ❑ file
- ❑ magnet
- ❑ 2 pieces of white paper

**procedure** ☆
1. Rub a nail over a file many times. Be sure to place a piece of paper under the file while you are rubbing the nail.
2. Place the second sheet of paper over the magnet.
3. Sprinkle the filings from the nail over the magnet.
4. Observe the pattern formed by the filings.

*Scrape a nail across the file.*

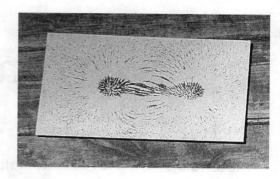

*The magnetic field of a magnet.*

**explanation ☆**  The iron filings from the nail line up along the force lines or *magnetic field* of the magnet. The field runs between the poles of the magnet. Try different shapes of magnets to see what their fields look like.

# 32
# A confused magnet

**objective** ☆  A magnet on a string will behave strangely around other magnets.

**materials** ☆
- ❏ 5 magnets about the same size (pieces of magnetic strips work, too)
- ❏ string
- ❏ tape

**procedure** ☆
1. Form a square with 4 of the magnets. Do not allow the ends of the magnets to touch.
2. Tape the last magnet to a piece of string.
3. Hold the string so that the hanging magnet is just above the other magnets.
4. Pull the magnet to one side and let it swing. What happens?

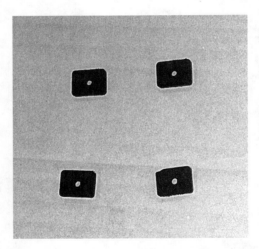

*Make a square out of magnets.*

*Swing the magnet on a string.*

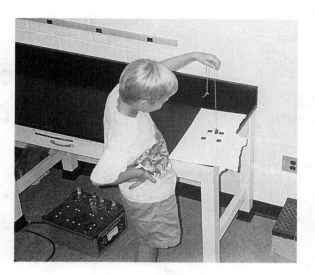

**explanation** ☆ As the magnet moves across the other magnets, it is attracted then repelled by the different poles of the other magnets.

# 33
# Making an electromagnet

**objective** ☆  You can use a nail or bolt to make an electromagnet.

**materials** ☆
- [ ] lantern battery
- [ ] nail or bolt, about 4 inches (10 cm) long
- [ ] insulated wire, about 3 feet (1 meter) long
- [ ] paper clips, thumbtacks, etc.

**procedure** ☆
1. Remove the insulation from about 1 to 2 inches (2 to 5 cm) of each end of wire.
2. Wrap the wire 40 to 50 times around the nail or bolt. Be sure to leave about 6 inches (15 cm) of wire at each end.
3. Touch the nail to a paper clip. Does the nail act as a magnet?
4. Attach the ends of the wires to the battery.
5. Touch the nail to the paper clip. Does the nail now act as a magnet?

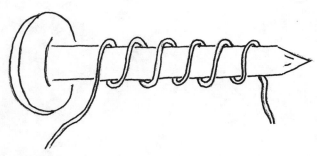

*Wrap wire around a nail.*

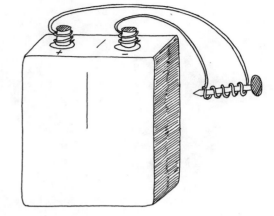

Attach the wire to the battery.

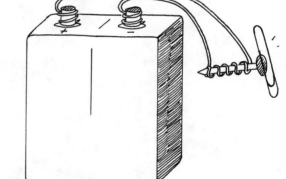

Use the nail as a magnet.

**explanation** ☆ The movement of electricity makes a *magnetic field*. When the nail was not hooked to the battery, the nail did not behave like a magnet. Only when electricity was moving around the nail did it behave like a magnet. Can you think of any uses for an electromagnet?

# Part 5
# Light

Light is another form of energy. In order for us to see an object light must be *reflected*, or bounced off, that object. Light can sometimes be reflected in such a way as to produce many images of the object. If the surface that light hits is not flat, the light is bent.

**important words**

☆ reflect

☆ concave

☆ convex

# 34
# Images in a spoon

**objective** ☆   Your face will look different depending on which side of the spoon you look at.

**materials** ☆   ❐ shiny spoon

**procedure** ☆   1. Hold the spoon so that the front of the spoon is facing you.
2. Look in the spoon. Is your image right-side-up or upside-down?
3. Turn the spoon around, and look in the spoon again. Is your image the same as it was when the spoon was turned the other way?

*Look at the front of a spoon.*

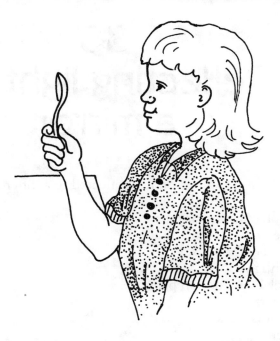

*Look at the back of a spoon.*

**explanation** ☆ The spoon acts like a curved mirror. Light is reflected off curved surfaces differently. When you look at the front surface of the spoon, it behaved like a *concave* (curving inward) mirror, and you were upside-down. When you looked at the back of the spoon, it behaved like a *convex* mirror, and you were right-side-up. Mirrors in fun houses are not flat but are curved in many different ways, so the image you see is very distorted.

# 35
# Reflecting light off a mirror

**objective** ☆ When light hits a mirror, it is reflected to a different position.

**materials** ☆
- ❏ small, rectangular mirror
- ❏ tape
- ❏ shoe box or book
- ❏ flashlight
- ❏ black construction paper
- ❏ scissors
- ❏ paper & pencil
- ❏ ruler

**procedure** ☆

1. Tape the mirror to the shoe box or book. The mirror should stand straight up.
2. Place the mirror on a sheet of paper.
3. Draw a line in front of the mirror. The line should be only as long as the mirror.

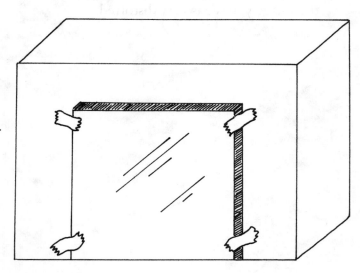

*Tape a mirror to a box.*

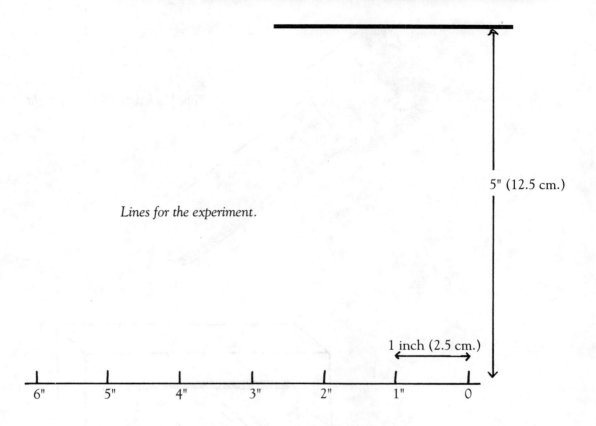

*Lines for the experiment.*

5" (12.5 cm.)

1 inch (2.5 cm.)

6"    5"    4"    3"    2"    1"    0

4. Place a mark on the middle of this line.
5. Draw a second line about 5 inches (12.5 cm) from the first line.
6. Starting in the middle of the second line, make four marks 1 inch (2.5 cm) apart.
7. Cut a piece of black paper just the size of end of the flashlight.
8. Make a small rectangular slit in the black paper.
9. Tape this black-paper circle to the flashlight. Be sure that the tape does not cover or touch the slit.
10. Darken the room.
11. Turn on the flashlight and place it on the first mark so the light hits the center of the mirror.
12. Mark on the right side of the large line the place where the light comes.

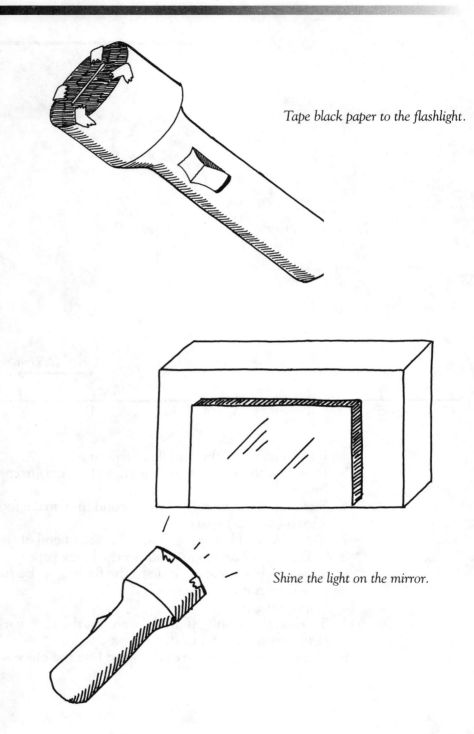

*Tape black paper to the flashlight.*

*Shine the light on the mirror.*

13. Repeat steps 11 and 12 for positions 2, 3, and 4.
14. Measure the distance from the center to each reflected line. What do you discover?

**explanation** ☆ The distance of the reflected light from the center should be the same distance from the center to the flashlight. When light hits a flat surface it is *reflected* at the same angle as it arrived from.

# 36
# Making many reflections

**objective** ☆ You will adjust 2 mirrors to get many reflections of an object.

**materials** ☆
- ❏ 2 small, identical-sized rectangular mirrors
- ❏ tape
- ❏ coin

**procedure** ☆
1. Tape the back of the mirrors together to make a mirror "book." The mirrors should be able to move like a hinge.
2. Place a coin on the X in the figure below.
3. Place the mirrors on the lines marked 1 in the illustration. How many images of the coin do you see?
4. Repeat step 3 for positions 2, 3, and 4.

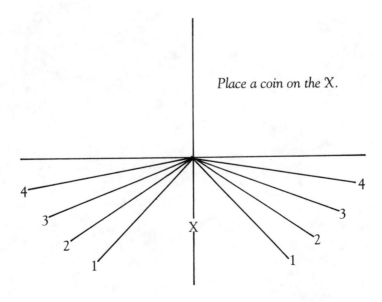

*Place a coin on the X.*

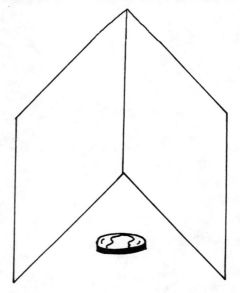

*The set up for this experiment.*

**explanation** ☆ An image of the coin appears in each mirror. These images are reflected into the other mirror, forming even more images. The smaller the angle between mirrors, as in 1, the more images that are formed.

# Part 6
# Heat

Heat is another form of energy. Heat moves from a hot area to a cooler area. Different materials allow heat to move at different speeds: an *insulator* slows down the movement of heat, and a *conductor* allows heat to move easily. In this section, you will examine different traits of heat.

**important words**
- ☆ conductor
- ☆ contract
- ☆ expand
- ☆ insulator

# 37
# The sagging wire

**objective** ☆ A wire, when heated, will sag.

**materials** ☆
- ❏ 2 plastic or glass soft-drink bottles
- ❏ thin copper wire, about 2 feet (60 cm) long
- ❏ string, about 12 inches (30 cm)
- ❏ paper clip or metal washer
- ❏ 2 identical-size candles
- ❏ water from faucet *or* sand
- ❏ clay (optional)
- ❏ matches

**procedure** ☆
1. Fill the bottles about half-full with water or sand.
2. Tie the wire to the bottles. The height of the wire should be such that the flame from the candle will touch the wire.
3. Move the bottles so the wire is tight.
4. Tie the paper clip or washer to the end of the string.
5. Tie the other end of the string to the middle of the wire. The paper clip should be about 1 inch (2.5 cm) above the counter.

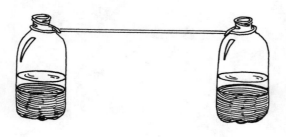

*Tie a wire to two bottles.*

*Attach a paper clip to the wire.*

6. Place the candles in clay so they won't fall over. Set the candles about 4 inches (10 cm) on either side of the string.
7. Have an adult light the candles. The flame from the candles should touch the wire.
8. Watch to see if the paper clip touches the table.
9. Blow out the candles. What happens to the position of the paper clip?

*Place candles under the wire.*

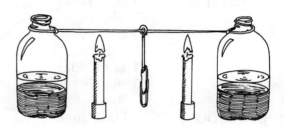

**explanation** ☆ Heat causes many metals to *expand*. As the wire expanded it became looser, and the paper clip touched the table. When the wire cooled, it contracted or shrank. The paper clip returned to the original position.

People sometimes use this principle to open jars. If you have trouble opening a jar, run the lid under hot water for 20 to 30 seconds. You then should be able to open the jar. For a similar experiment see experiment 38.

# 38
# The falling coin

**objective** ☆ A coin will fall from a wire clamp when the wire is heated. *Note:* You should do experiment 37 before doing this experiment.

**materials** ☆
- [ ] metal coat hanger
- [ ] pliers
- [ ] coin
- [ ] candle
- [ ] pot holder
- [ ] matches

**procedure** ☆

1. Have an adult cut a coat hanger so you have a piece of wire about 1 foot (30 cm) long.
2. Bend the coat hanger into the shape of a triangle. The ends of the wire should touch.
3. Place a coin between the ends of the wire.
4. Use a pot holder to grasp the pliers. Then use the pliers to grasp the wire.
5. Place the candle on the counter and have an adult light the candle.

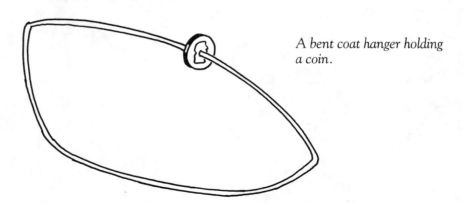

*A bent coat hanger holding a coin.*

6. Place the side of the triangle that is opposite the coin in the flame.
7. Observe what happens to the coin after a few minutes. Why do you think this happened?

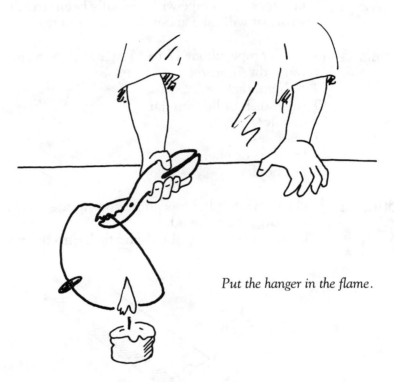

*Put the hanger in the flame.*

**explanation** ☆ As you saw in experiment 37, heat makes metals expand. The heated wire expanded, and was no longer able to hold the coin.

# 39
# Falling thumbtacks

**objective** ☆ Thumbtacks on a pipe will gradually begin to fall off. *Note:* This experiment will take about 20 to 30 minutes.

**materials** ☆
- ❏ copper pipe, about 12 to 15 inches (30-38 cm) long; available in hardware stores
- ❏ 5 thumbtacks
- ❏ small dish or lid from jar
- ❏ candle
- ❏ matches
- ❏ tweezers or pliers
- ❏ pot holder

**procedure** ☆
1. Have an adult light a candle and tip the candle so some of the wax drips into the lid.
2. Using tweezers, dip the thumbtack into the hot wax.

*Drip wax into a lid.*

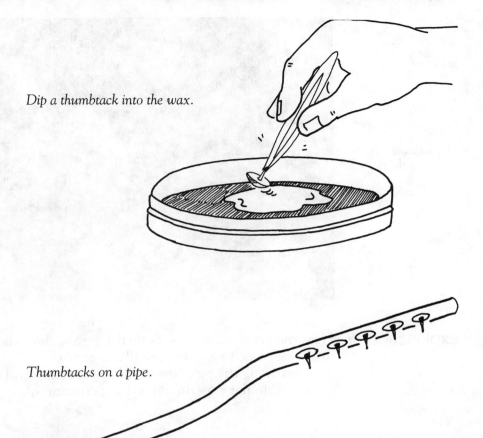

*Dip a thumbtack into the wax.*

*Thumbtacks on a pipe.*

3. Place the thumbtacks on the pipe. The tacks should start about 1 inch (2.5 cm) from the end of the pipe, and should be spaced about 1 inch (2.5 cm) apart.
4. Allow the wax to cool 10 to 15 minutes.
5. Hold the empty end of the pipe in the pot holder.
6. If the candle is out, have an adult light the candle.
7. Place the other end of the pipe in the flame of the candle.
8. Observe what happens to the tacks. Do they all fall off at the same time?

*Place the pipe in
the flame.*

**explanation** ☆   Heat travels along metals. Something that allows heat to move
from one place to another is called a *conductor*. As the heat
traveled along the pipe, the wax began to melt and the tacks fell
off. For a similar experiment, see experiment 40.

# 40
# More falling thumbtacks

**objective** ☆    You and a friend can have a race to see which wire loses its thumbtacks first. *Note:* This experiment requires two people, will take 20 to 30 minutes, and should be done after experiment 39.

**materials** ☆
- ❏ 2 different wires, about 12 inches (30 cm) long (a copper wire and a coat hanger work well)
- ❏ 4 or 6 thumbtacks
- ❏ small dish or lid from jar
- ❏ tweezers or pliers
- ❏ candle
- ❏ matches
- ❏ 2 pot holders

**procedure** ☆

1. Have an adult cut a coat hanger to make a piece of wire about 12 inches (30 cm) long.
2. Have an adult light the candle and tip the candle so the wax drips into the lid. (See experiment 39.)
3. Using tweezers, dip the tacks into the hot wax. (See experiment 39.)
4. Place 2 or 3 thumbtacks on each wire. The tacks should be about 2 inches (5 cm) apart and 2 inches (5 cm) from one end of the pipe. Allow the wax to cool 15 to 20 minutes.

*Two different wires with tacks attached.*

5. Grasp the end of each wire with a pot holder.
6. Have an adult light the candle again.
7. Place the ends of the wires in the flame at the same time. Did the tacks start to fall at the same time? Why do you think they started to fall?

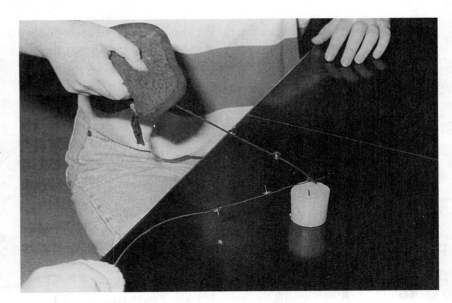

*Hold the wires in the flame.*

**explanation ☆**   As you saw in the last experiment, metals conduct heat. As the heat moves along the wire, the wax melts. Different metals conduct heat at different rates. Copper conducts better than steel or aluminum, so the tacks fell off the copper wire first.

Because copper is such a good conductor of heat, it is often used on the bottom of pots and pans. Food in copper pans is heated more quickly than food in other kinds of pans.

# 41
# Wet or dry pot holder?

**objective** ☆    You will see that a dry pot holder is always better than a wet one.

**materials** ☆
- ❏ pan
- ❏ spoon
- ❏ pot holder
- ❏ water from faucet

**procedure** ☆

1. Have an adult heat a pan on the stove for 5 to 10 minutes.
2. Cover your hand with the pot holder and touch the side of the pan. Do you feel any heat?
3. Sprinkle some water on the pot holder so part of it is slightly damp. **Caution!** Do not make the pot holder completely wet.
4. Touch the pan again with the damp part of the pot holder. Do you feel the heat now? What did the water do to the pot holder?

*Touch the pan with the pot holder.*

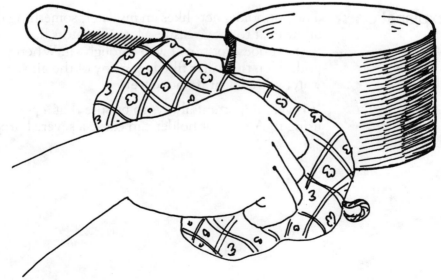

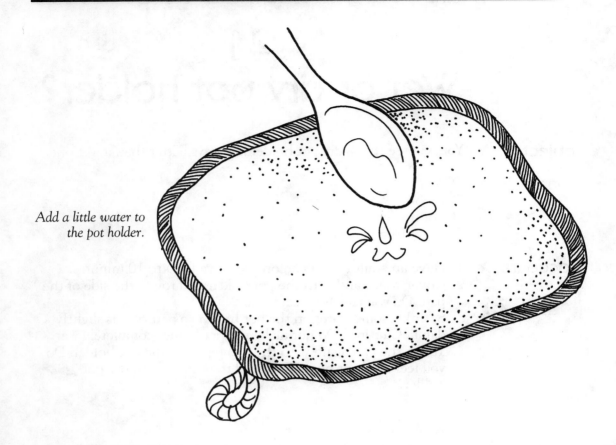

*Add a little water to the pot holder.*

**explanation** ☆ The pot holder acts likes an *insulator*, something that does not allow heat to move easily. Most insulators have many air spaces, for heat does not travel well through air. When you moistened the potholder, the water filled up many of the air spaces. Therefore, water allows heat to move well.

It is very important always to be sure that a pot holder is dry before using it. A wet pot holder can cause a severe burn.

# 42
# Making a coat hanger hot

**objective** ☆ Quickly bending a coat hanger will make it become hot.

**materials** ☆ ☐ metal coat hanger
☐ pliers or wire cutters (for the adult to use)

**procedure** ☆ 1. Have an adult cut open a metal coat hanger with the pliers.
2. Rapidly bend the coat hanger back and forth 5 or 6 times.
3. Touch the hanger where it has been bent. How does the coat hanger feel?

*Bend the coat hanger.*

*Touch the bent coat hanger.*

**explanation** ☆ Bending the hanger makes the molecules in the hanger rub together. This rubbing releases heat and the wire becomes hot. You can do a similar thing by rubbing 2 wires or pieces of metal against each other many times.

Sometimes rubbing two metal objects together can create so much heat that sparks are released and a fire can start. For this reason, oil is used in a car's engine to prevent metals from rubbing against each other and becoming too hot.

# 43
# How fast does ice melt?

**objective** ☆ You will compare how fast ice cubes and crushed ice melt. *Note: This experiment will take about 60 to 90 minutes.*

**materials** ☆
- ☐ 2 ice cubes, approximately the same size
- ☐ 2 identical-sized glasses or jars
- ☐ hammer (for the adult to use)
- ☐ plastic sandwich bag or piece of plastic wrap
- ☐ watch
- ☐ paper & pencil

**procedure** ☆
1. Place one ice cube in a plastic bag and close the bag.
2. Have an adult use the hammer to crush the ice.
3. Put all the crushed ice into a glass. Place the cube of ice in the other glass. Place both glasses on the counter.
4. Look at each glass every 5 minutes.
5. Record the time it took for all the ice in each glass to melt.

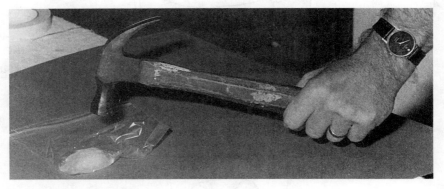

*Have an adult crush the ice.*

*Place crushed ice in a glass.*

*Place an ice cube in a glass.*

**explanation** ☆   Ice melts because heat from the air moves to the ice. If ice is in many small pieces, like the crushed ice, more of the surface is exposed to the heat. The cube had much less surface area exposed to the heat, so it took longer to melt.

Which do you think will dissolve faster, a sugar cube in a cup of water or a teaspoon of loose sugar in a cup of water? Based on the results of this experiment, can you explain why mittens keep your hands warmer than gloves in the winter time?

# Glossary

**amplify**  to make stronger or louder

**bass**  low sounds

**circuit**  a complete path through which electricity can move

**concave**  curving inward like the front surface of a spoon

**conductor**  an object or material that allows heat or electricity to travel through it

**contract**  to get smaller or come closer together

**convex**  curving outward, like the back of a spoon

**expand**  to get larger or move farther apart

**frequency**  how fast something happens within a given amount of time; usually used to describe how fast air is vibrating in each second

**friction**  rubbing together of two or more objects, usually resulting in the object slowing down or becoming hotter

**gravity**  a force of attraction between two objects, usually responsible for objects falling in a downward direction

**inclined plane**  a ramp that allows less energy to be used in moving an object to a higher position

**inertia**  tendency of moving objects to keep moving and resting objects to continue at rest

**insulator**  object or material that prevents the flow of heat or electricity

**magnetic field**  area of force produced by a magnet

**molecule**  smallest part of a compound that can exist freely but still have all the properties of that compound

**pendulum**  object hanging at end of string or wire that moves back and forth

**pitch**  a trait of sound that depends on the frequency of vibration

**reflect**  to bounce off of

**siphon**  pipe or tube used to move liquid from a high position to a lower position

**treble**  high-pitched sounds

**vacuum**  absence of air

**vibrate**  to shake or move back and forth

**volume**  amount of three-dimensional space taken up by a solid, liquid, or gas

# Index